# Growing Up

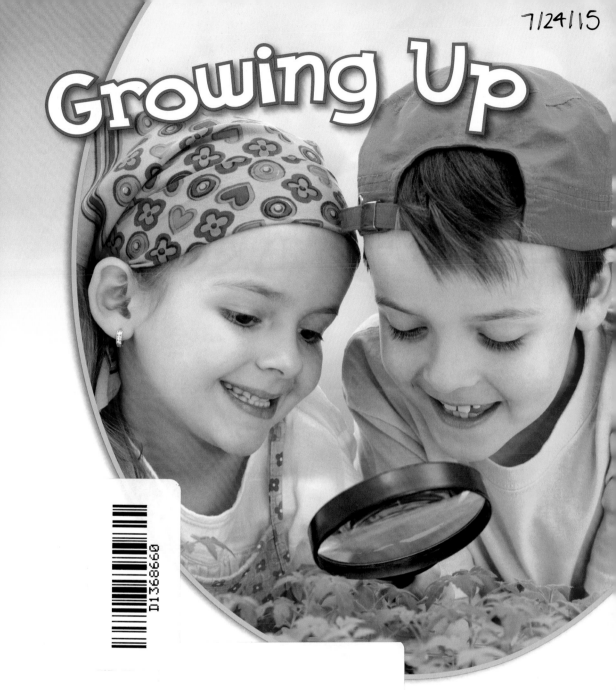

## Dona Herweck Rice

Every living thing
**grows up.**

It **changes** as it grows.

It gets bigger.

Sometimes, it gets
much bigger!

It gets faster.

Sometimes, it gets much faster!

It may get more hair.

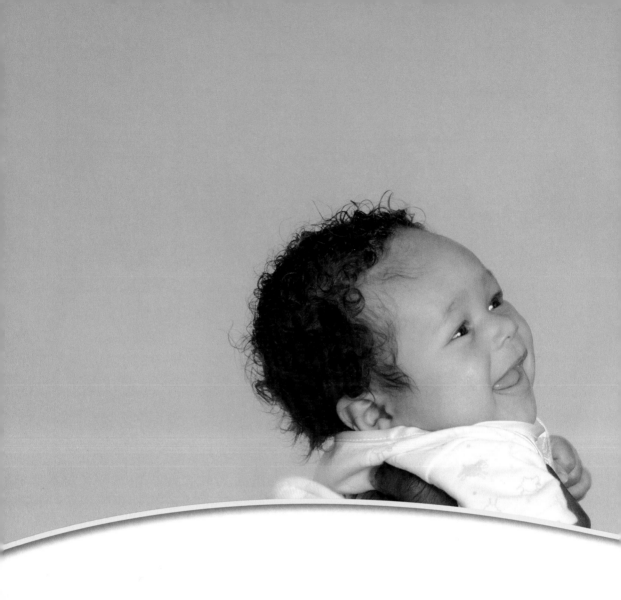

It may get less hair!

It may know more things.

It may do more
things.

Change is a big part
of growing up.

# Let's Do Science!

How do living things change over time?
Try this!

## What to Get

- ❏ paper and pencil
- ❏ plant
- ❏ tape measure

# What to Do

**1** Get a calendar.

**2** Have an adult help you measure the plant.

**3** Write the plant's height on the calendar.

**4** Do this each week for a month. At the end of the month, what changed?

# Glossary

**changes**—becomes different in some way

**grows up**—becomes an adult

# Index

# Your Turn!

Look at photos of you
from the time you were
born until now. Draw
pictures to show how you
have changed.

## Consultants

**Sally Creel, Ed.D.**
Curriculum Consultant

**Leann Iacuone, M.A.T., NBCT, ATC**
Riverside Unified School District

**Jill Tobin**
California Teacher of the Year
Semi-Finalist
Burbank Unified School District

### Publishing Credits

Conni Medina, M.A.Ed., *Managing Editor*

Lee Aucoin, *Creative Director*

Diana Kenney, M.A.Ed., NBCT, *Senior Editor*

Lynette Tanner, *Editor*

Lexa Hoang, *Designer*

Hillary Dunlap, *Photo Editor*

Rachelle Cracchiolo, M.S.Ed., *Publisher*

**Image Credits:** Cover & pp.1, 4, 8, 24 iStock; p.9 Richard Kolar/age fotostock; p.22 Cultura Creative/Alamy; p.12 Radius Images/Alamy; p.17 UpperCut Images/Alamy; p.14 Elmar Herz/imagebroker; p.10 Splash News/Newscom; pp.18–19 (illustrations) J.J. Rudisill; all other images from Shutterstock.

### Library of Congress Cataloging-in-Publication Data

Rice, Dona, author.
  Growing up / Dona Herweck Rice.
    pages cm
    Summary: "It is time to learn how living things grow and change."—Provided by publisher.
  Audience: K to grade 3.
  Includes index.
  ISBN 978-1-4807-4524-7 (pbk.) —
  ISBN 978-1-4807-5133-0 (ebook)
1.  Growth--Juvenile literature. 2.  Life cycles (Biology)—Juvenile literature. 3.  Readers (Primary)  I. Title.
  QH511.R623 2015
  571.8—dc23

                                    2014008924

### Teacher Created Materials

5301 Oceanus Drive
Huntington Beach, CA  92649-1030
http://www.tcmpub.com
**ISBN 978-1-4807-4524-7**
© 2015 Teacher Created Materials, Inc.